Polly Finds Treasure

Jann Weeratunga

Copyright © 2019 Jann Weeratunga

All rights reserved.

ISBN:
ISBN-13:

DEDICATION

To Tonia, who has encouraged me to write from the start, thank you for always being there and believing in me, even when I doubted myself. To all the friends who have shown me so much support with the production of my first book Polly's Piralympics, thank you.

And to Auntie Pauline and Uncle Bill for always being in my life and to my mum always my biggest fan. Love you mum.

ACKNOWLEDGEMENTS

To Margaret forever my sounding board on the first drafts.
To Anivesh for believing in me and publishing my book
Dalene for her patience with my constant questions when setting up my Facebook page: Polly's Feather Club

CONTENTS

Polly Rescues Roger

The Empty Ship

Where's all the Treasure?

The Ghost of Blackbeard

The Rescue

Polly to the Rescue

Message in a Bottle

Skull Island

Polly Finds Treasure

Polly Rescues Roger

Polly the Parrot found Roger the Rat on deck.

"You want to play Hide 'n' Seek Roger?"

Polly the Parrot and Roger the Rat loved this game, the Pirates too often joined in. They would hide in the crow's nest, inside barrels, behind the sails, under the ropes or behind the ship's wheel. Captain Hake would grin, his big gold-toothed grin when he saw them playing with the crew.

'*All's right in the pirate world,*' he thought to himself. His crew were happy.

Polly covered her eye with her wing. Her blind eye was covered with a special pirate patch Make had made for her.

"6, 7, 8, 9... 10. Coming!"

She opened her one good eye and started running around the deck on her short legs. Soon, she had found most of the crew, but where was Roger the Rat? Just as she spotted him sitting near the end of the ship's plank (used for bad pirates when they had to 'walk the plank'). A huge seagull swooped down towards him.

Polly the Parrot didn't hesitate, her friend was in danger. She raced along the deck and out onto the gangplank as fast as her legs would carry her, squawking, shrieking and screaming a warning to Roger the Rat.

Hearing all the commotion, Captain Hake left the ship's wheel and ran to the edge of the poop deck, just in time to see Polly the Parrot running out onto the gangplank at full speed.

"Polly, wait up," cried a pirate.

"Wait, Polly."

"Hold on there girl."

"Polly, ya can nae fly girl." Captain Hake cried out. "Polly NOOOO!"

But, it was too late. Roger the Rat had already jumped when he saw the seagull swooping down on him. In a split second he decided water was the better option than being snapped up in a beak, so, he jumped off the end of the plank.

Polly the Parrot oblivious to the shouting from her Captain and the crew ran at full speed towards Roger the Rat. Just as she saw him jump off the end of the plank she shouted.

"Don't worry Roger I'll save you!"

There was no time to think, she ran straight off the end of the plank. At this point, gravity took over and she started to plummet towards the sea. Roger the Rat was just ahead of her. She reached out her feet and grabbed him by the tail. But, they were still heading for the water very quickly.

Meanwhile, back on the deck of the Thistle, Captain Hake had reached the gunnels and stared out over the edge. He tried in vain to spot Polly.

There she was, holding on to Roger the rat's tail.

"Spread your wings, Polly me girl, spread 'em pet."

Somehow, Polly the Parrot managed to hear Captain Hake. She lifted her wings and spread them out as wide as she could. Then something happened. She could feel the wind rushing under her wings, and slowing her descent.

"Now flap Polly, FLAP ME GIRL."

Just before they hit the sea, Polly the Parrot flapped her wings. They felt strong, and she slowly started to rise above the waves.

"I'm flying Roger, I'm flying!"

Yes, Polly the Parrot in the face of danger had learnt to fly.

"I'm glad about that, wondered when it would happen," said Roger the Rat, relieved that she had saved them both from a watery end.

Polly flapped and flapped and slowly they rose into the air. She circled around the main mast, up to the crow's nest and then did another loop.

"Look Cap'n. I'm flying."

Captain Hake was busy wiping a tear away from his eye. He was sure that she was a goner, and the relief was almost too much.

The crew whooped and cheered as she flew down to the deck and rather heavily crash landed.

"OK, so I need to work on the landings," she chirped.

Captain Hake ran forward and picked them both up, he laughed and cried at the same time.

"Ya did it, Polly, ya flew me hearty."

He was so happy, he ordered double rations of lemonade and chocolate biscuits to be served to the whole crew. Everyone danced, sang and celebrated way into the evening.

Roger the Rat went up to Polly the Parrot when things had quietened down a bit.

"Thanks, Polly. I thought for sure I was a goner."

"Not on my watch, Roger."

With that, the two curled up together in an empty barrel and fell fast asleep. That night, Roger the Rat dreamt of making a 'thank you' cake for Polly the Parrot, and, Polly the Parrot dreamt of flying over the jungles of Africa, searching for her family and friends.

Polly was very brave to jump off the plank to save Roger the Rat. Have you ever done anything that was brave?

Draw a picture of you as a pirate superhero.

The Empty Ship

Months passed and Polly the Parrot became the inseparable friend of Captain Hake. She would sit on his shoulder as he walked around the deck. Soon she was very fond of her Captain. She would do anything for him or a member of his crew, they had all been so kind to her and made her feel at home.

One day the wind dropped to a whisper, but the solar sails propelled them along at a steady pace. Then Wake, who was awake for once in the crow's nest, spotted a ship on the starboard side of the Thistle.

"Ship Ahoy."

First Mate Jake was on duty. He quickly held the telescope to his eye.

"It can nae be possible," First Mate Jake stammered, hardly able to believe his eyes. He peered down the telescope again. "Polly, get the Cap'n, he's gonna want to see this."

Polly found Captain Hake sitting on a deck chair sunbathing outside his cabin.

"Ship Ahoy on the starboard side, Cap'n."

Captain Hake quickly clunked his way up onto the poop deck and alongside his First Mate, Jake.

"Take a look, Cap'n."

Captain Hake peered down the telescope through his one good eye.

"By jingers, it cannae be!" He said. "First Mate Jake, take Take, Snake, Rake and Drake in the rowboat over to that there ship and check it out. Be sharp mind, ya nae know who you may come across."

First Mate Jake ordered the men into the small rowing boat.

"Are we seriously going to board that ship?" Asked Take as he took a deep breath.

The ship they had spotted was now only a few hundred meters away and looked empty. Grey tattered sails hung limply from its masts, and spiders' webs were strung like net curtains all over the decks. The cannons sat rusting on their carriages and odd ropes and cleats squeaked and swung even though there was no breeze. A threadbare Jolly Roger fluttered gently at the top of the main mast.

"Do, do, do we have to go on board First Mate?" A rather nervous Rake asked.

"Aye, the Cap'n has bid it. And ay dinni want any scaredy cats, so be brave now."

Though First Mate Jake was as nervous as the rest of the crew, he wanted to appear brave so they would respect him.

The ship they had encountered was none other than the 'Queen Anne's Revenge.' Now a ghost ship. All had thought she had been run aground by Captain Blackbeard in 1718, but no-one had ever discovered her remains. It was rumoured she still sailed the seven seas with a ghost crew.

First Mate Jake steered the rowing boat alongside. In nothing more than a whisper, he called out,

"Is there anyone aboard?"

Silence.

"Ok, no-one home. Let's get back to our own ship." Rake said quickly.

Then, First Mate Jake's phone rang.

"Well?"

It was Captain Hake.

"Er-hem, nothin', Cap'n. There's no one here. Shall we come back now?"

"Nae, board her man. See what she's carrying."

First Mate Jake instructed his men to tie up their rowing boat and get ready to board the ship.

The pirates were scared to go aboard Captain Blackbeard's ship because it was a ghost ship. Draw your ghost ship.

Where is all the Treasure?

Meanwhile, Captain Hake spoke quietly to Polly the Parrot.

"What d'ya think Polly? Is it her?"

"Aye Cap'n I think it is," Polly replied. "D'ya want me to fly over an' take a wee look?"

Polly the Parrot had learnt on the Internet that pirates for years had searched for the Queen Anne's Revenge. The notorious, Captain Blackbeard, fiercest captain to have ever sailed the Seven Seas was supposed to have had treasure filled to the gunnels of his ship when she was last seen.

"Ok Polly, but be alert me pet, I dinni want to see you hurt. Come back at the first sign of danger."

Polly confidently flew over to the Queen Anne's Revenge. She circled the ship twice before descending to the yardarm. There she perched and took a good look around.

'*Hmm, no-one about. That's good.*'

Then she fluttered down to the poop deck. The ship's wheel swayed with the to and fro motion of the sea, and the ship's compass just spun around in circles.

'*Odd,*' she thought.

Then, Polly, the Parrot hopped down onto the main deck. There were spider's webs everywhere, but she carefully manoeuvred passed them. She hopped on down the ladder that led below decks and to the galley. The ship appeared to be totally empty, not a sausage stirred.

Polly the Parrot stuck her head out of a porthole and spoke to First Mate Jake.

"Okay, seems quiet enough, but keep clear of the spider's webs, I just have a funny feeling about them."

First Mate Jake ordered his men to board the Queen Anne's Revenge, but not before giving them, Polly the Parrots, warning.

Rake, Take, Snake and Drake boarded the ghost ship. They tippy-toed along the deck, weaved and ducked the spider's webs, then made their way below decks.

"Make a thorough search of the hold," First Mate Jake instructed, "and if you find anything, DON'T TOUCH IT!"

Polly the Parrot flew up to meet First Mate Jake as he was about to enter Captain Blackbeard's quarters.

"Better look lively Polly. I dinni want to be here any longer than needs be."

They both searched the cabin, but there was no gold. Only a few old charts were strewn across the table and a bottle of pop rolled from one side to the other with the rocking motion of the ship.

"Well, it looks like Captain Blackbeard took all his treasure with him Polly."

Then, Polly the Parrot spied a rolled up parchment inside a bottle.

"Maybe not. First Mate Jake, what d'ya think that is?" She pointed to the bottle with the tip of her wing.

"I dinni know Polly. Let's take it for the Cap'n to look at."

First Mate Jake picked up the bottle and tucked it into his shirt and they started to leave the room. Just as they closed the door to Captain Blackbeard's cabin, there was shouting and a hullabaloo below decks.

"I told those stupid pirates not to touch anything," cried First Mate Jake.

First Mate Jake and Polly the Parrot searched Captain Blackbeard's cabin. Draw a picture of that cabin.

The Ghost of Blackbeard

Below deck, Take, Rake, Snake and Drake carefully hunted for treasure. They checked down the cannons, under the coiled ropes, inside all the barrels and even behind the anchor, but there was no gold.

"Fine pirate shhhhhhip thissss issss wi' nae gold on board," hissed Snake. The hissing sound was made through a gap in his teeth and was pretty scary.

"Well, shall we head back on deck?"

Rake still felt very nervous and wanted to get off this ship as quickly as he possibly could. But, as they walked to the stairs Take spotted something shiny in the corner, behind the wheel of a cannon.

"You go on, I'll just be a jiff."

Take walked closer, as he did, he saw that the shiny object was, in fact, a gold goblet. He looked around him quickly.

'*No-one will notice if I take this,*' he thought and reached forward for the goblet. Just as he was about to take it, Take sneezed – '*Too much dust on his old ship.*'

Accidentally his hand knocked the goblet. There was a rumble, sploosh, and ROAR as a hole appeared in the ship's hull and in walked Captain Blackbeard himself.

"Be tryin' to steal me treasure was ye?" Captain Blackbeard's voice boomed over the gushing water.

Take, who was going to take the goblet shook his head in denial, but, knew he was telling a lie and quickly changed it to a nod.

Hearing the noise behind them, the rest of the crew turned and drew their swords, but in doing so, Rake's sword raked against one of the webs, slicing in through. Suddenly, ghost pirates drifted up through the floor and in through the hull of the ship. They were in a tight jam.

Above deck, First Mate Jake ordered Polly the Parrot to return to the Thistle and tell Captain Hake that something was up and that they needed help. Polly flew off at top speed, she glanced behind her just in time to see the rest of the crew emerge from below deck, chased by ghostly pirates wielding swords and cutlasses.

Captain Hake had already heard the boom and commotion and had given orders to get the Thistle underway. She sailed at full speed towards the Queen Anne's Revenge and met Polly the Parrot halfway.

'Thank goodness Make was able to make those special solar sails,' thought Polly the Parrot, *'gives the Cap'n immediate speed.'*

Yes, thank goodness.

By cutting through the spider's web, Rake had inadvertently set off a booby trap designed to wake the sleeping ghost crew of Captain Blackbeard if anyone should come looking for their treasure. Now, Captain Hake's crew was up on the deck, but surrounded by fearless ghost pirates, who looked - well horrible.

The crew had drawn their swords and were standing in a circle back to back and ready to defend themselves. To one side Captain Blackbeard put his huge hands on his hips and said.

"Who are you, and why have ye woken me an' me crew?"

First Mate Jake faced the formidable giant and tried not to show that he was a little afraid.

"We apologise for waking you, Captain Blackbeard. It's just your ship hasn't been seen for almost three hundred years, and we..." his voice tailed off.

"Ya what? I'll tell ya what. Ya thought seein' as how me ship was unmanned, yas thought yas would come steal me treasure."

First Mate Jake knew this was true, but didn't want to admit to it. Take who had taken the goblet was trying to poke it under a rope with his foot but was spotted by Captain Blackbeard.

"There, see!" Captain Blackbeard pointed a huge finger straight at Take.

Take gulped, he knew he shouldn't have taken the goblet, but he just couldn't help himself, after all, he was a pirate.

"Well, a bounty has to be paid in blood for the crime," Captain Blackbeard continued, "run them through me hearties!"

Suddenly the menacing ghost crew lunged forward and started to attack Captain Hake's crew. Swords clashed, as the ghostly steel raked across the newer lighter modern swords. Snake hissed as a sword sliced through his t-shirt.

"That's it," he said, "that was my new t-shirt, and I only bought it last shore leave."

They fought hard against the ghostly aggressors, but it was no good. Slowly, Captain Hake's crew was being pushed towards the plank.

"There's nothing for it lads, out along the plank."

First Mate Jake could see no other means of them escaping with their lives. If they remained on board the ghost ship, the ghost crew would surely run them through. The crew did as ordered and stepped out onto the plank.

The ghostly crew are very scary. I think I would be afraid of them, wouldn't you?

Draw a picture of some of Captain Blackbeard's crew.

The Rescue

Meanwhile, the Thistle was sailing at full steam towards the Queen Anne's Revenge. Captain Hake shouted out orders and his crew obeyed instantly.

"Be sharp now. Their lives depend on us," he bellowed from the poop deck as he steered the Thistle straight at the other ship.

"Will we make it, d'ya think Polly? I'd hate to lose that bunch of scallywags."

"Aye Cap'n. We'll make it," encouraged Polly the Parrot. *'We have to,'* she thought secretly. Polly the Parrot had come a long way from hating the Two-Legged Destroyers, and now these pirates were her friends. But it was going to be tight. There would be no second chances for a rescue of this type.

Captain Hake manoeuvred the Thistle like a dream, at the last minute he brought the Thistle around and was parallel to the Queen Anne's Revenge.

"Jump!"

First Mate Jake looked up to see the Thistle just at the end of the plank.

"Right mates, yas heard the Cap'n. Jump to the Thistle."

On board the Thistle the remaining crew were ready to catch First Mate Jake and the rest of the crew as they jumped the gap that separated the two ships. The men leapt to safety like rats deserting a sinking ship, which is indeed what the Queen Anne's Revenge was doing - sinking.

Last, still standing on the plank was Take. He still had the golden goblet in his hand and a sword in the other and was fighting to the last to give the rest of the crew time to jump to safety.

"Jump man!" Ordered Captain Hake. A lump in his throat as he realised the peril his crewmate was in.

Take was hopelessly outnumbered, but he fought on bravely.

"JUMP MAN. I CANNAE HOLD HER ALONGSIDE ANY LONGER."

The solar panels were driving the sails and engine of the Thistle on, and there were no brakes on this ship.

Take was determined that no ghost pirates would jump across the plank and had decided to defend the plank with his life.

"It's Ok Cap'n," he shouted bravely as the Thistle started to pull away from the sinking Queen Anne's Revenge.

Soon it would be too late.

But still Take fought on.

Captain Hake has to sail his ship quickly to rescue his crew. Draw a picture of his crew standing on the gangplank fighting the ghost pirates.

Polly to the Rescue

Polly the Parrot in the meantime had guessed what Take was up to. He blamed himself for triggering Captain Blackbeard's appearance by moving the goblet and had decided to sacrifice himself to save the rest of the crew.

'*Not on my watch,*' thought Polly the Parrot.

She really liked Take. He had often taken her with him up into the crow's nest to wake up Wake when he had fallen asleep. They would sit up there and chat for hours until they were missed. He had also taken her part when the two pirates had teased her, quickly calling it to the attention of Captain Hake. Take too hated bullies.

Polly the Parrot flew down to the Thistle's rowing boat which was still attached to the Queen Anne's Revenge. With her beak, she managed to untie the knot holding it to the ship and flew with the rope in her beak towards the Thistle.

The Thistle was now a safe distance away and Take was still fighting single-handed on the plank for his life.

"Gold stolen, must be gold returned," bellowed Captain Blackbeard from the gunnels.

By now the Queen Anne's Revenge had started to list heavily and Take had trouble keeping his balance.

"Jump, Take, NOW!" Screeched Polly the Parrot.

Take didn't think. He just jumped. As he did so, Polly the Parrot nipped the hand that held the goblet. In pain Take let go of the goblet as he fell towards the sea.

POOF. The Queen Anne's Revenge was gone. She had disappeared. Captain Blackbeard, his full crew and ship, were all gone.

Take instead of falling into the sea to become shark bait, had, in fact fallen rather heavily into the rowing boat and knocked himself out.

Polly the Parrot had been clever enough to tie the end of the rope to the Thistle and the little rowing boat was now being trailed along behind her.

Polly the Parrot flew back to Captain Hake. He had a tear in his eye and many of his crew were snivelling and crying.

"He gave his life for us."

"Aye, he was a brave pirate."

"True, true."

"It'll nae be the same wi'out him."

The crew lamented the loss of Take, he had always been a popular pirate on board the Thistle.

"He was a good man Polly," Captain Hake whispered to his best friend, as she landed lightly on his shoulder.

"He still is Cap'n."

"What d'ya mean Polly? He went down fighting and we all saw the Queen Anne's Revenge disappear."

"Aye Cap'n, but look to the stern."

Captain Hake looked out of the back of the ship and saw the rowing boat with Take, out for the count being towed along.

"Ya little beauty Polly."

Captain Hake was ecstatic and immediately gave orders for Take to be brought on board.

Yes, Polly the Parrot's father had been right. Polly the Parrot really was the most incredibly clever little bird.

Polly was very clever. She rescued Take in a barrel attached to the back of Captain Hake's ship by a rope. Why don't you draw a picture of this on some paper?

Message in a Bottle

After things quietened down, and Take was back on board and in his bunk recovering, Polly the Parrot drew Captain Hake to one side.

"Meet me in your cabin Cap'n," she whispered.

'What's this all about? Polly has never been so secretive,' thought Captain Hake as he made his way to his quarters.

He closed the door.

"Right Polly. What's this all about?"

In the Captain's cabin was also First Mate Jake. He held out the bottle that he and Polly the Parrot had discovered on board Captain Blackbeard's ship.

"Think ya might like to take a wee look at this Cap'n."

Jake handed over the bottle containing the old parchment. Captain Hake managed to shake the parchment free of the bottle and opened it.

"It's a treasure map, Polly," exclaimed Captain Hake.

Sure enough, there in his hands was Captain Blackbeard's treasure map.

"Is nae that Skull Island?" Asked First Mate Jake.

"Aye."

"Out of the frying pan and into the fire." First Mate Jake muttered under his breath.

"What's that?" Questioned Captain Hake.

"Ay, said, then shall I set a course for Skull Island Cap'n?"

"Aye. Full steam ahead First Mate Jake. Let's be seeing some life in the crew. It will be good to get their minds off that there ghost ship too."

So, they set sail for Skull Island.

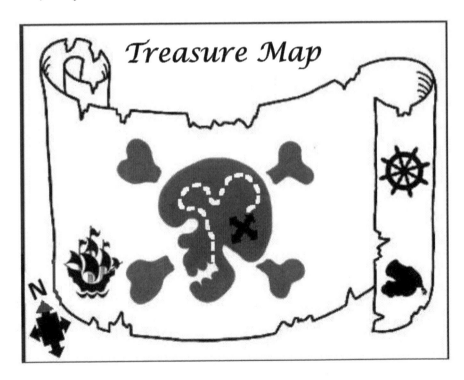

Draw your own treasure map on some paper and show your mum/dad or teacher

Skull Island

Skull Island was so named because it was the shape of a skull, but many of the pirates didn't like going there as they thought it was bad luck. Captain Hake knew this, but pushed his men to go there never the less.

They parked in Teeth Bay and rowed ashore.

Half the crew led by First Mate Jake were to fetch fresh water, fruits and anything else they could scavenge. The balance consisted of Take, Flake, Shake, and Wake, who accompanied Captain Hake and Polly the Parrot. They followed the map until eventually, they came upon an X marked on the ground.

"This must be it, Polly."

Captain Hake rubbed his hands and gave a gold toothy grin. But instead of having to dig for the treasure they simply had to open a trap door. Yes, the X on the map had led them to a trap door on the ground.

Captain Hake instructed Wake to stand guard over the trap door.

"And stay awake!"

Polly Finds Treasure

He then led the way, with his pocket torch run by Dappacell batteries, so that the beam would last a long time, down the stairs. At the bottom, there were three doors. On the first was a picture of a baby. On the second a picture of a person in a wheelchair, and on the third a picture of a man standing next to a woman.

"Which one do we choose Polly?"

"I don't know Cap'n."

"Ok, Flake open a door," instructed Captain Hake.

Flake opened the door marked with a baby. There, packed to the ceiling was a room full of boxes of baby clothes.

"What kinda treasure is this?"

Captain Hake rubbed his head with his hook and shrugged.

"Ok Take, you take a turn."

Take had made a full recovery from the bang on the head that had knocked him out earlier, except that he could remember nothing about the ghost ship. He stepped forward and opened the door with the lady and man on it.

A TOILET!

Take and the rest of the crew nervously laughed.

"Ok, so the last door then."

Captain Hake opened this himself. Instead of finding gold, silver and jewels piled up, there were instead prosthetic arms, blades and racing wheelchairs.

'What odd treasure.' thought Polly the Parrot?

"Well, at least it is something Cap'n."

She had seen the frown of disappointment cross Captain Hake's face.

"Aye, 'tis that Polly. Right, Shake, shake a leg, get back to the rest of the crew and get them back here to load this lot aboard me ship."

Shake went to say something, but changed his mind and left shaking his head.

The treasure of baby clothes and prosthetic arms, blades and racing wheelchairs were loaded aboard the Thistle. Soon Captain Hake, Polly the Parrot and the crew were sailing the Seven Seas, looking for another adventure.

What would they do with their recent bounty, yes, what indeed?

Captain Hake had a very special ship with lifts and solar panel sails. If you had a pirate ship what would it look like? Name the special things that you would have on your ship. Draw it here.

Other books by Jann Weeratunga
Available through Amazon.com and Amazon.UK

How Polly Became a Parrot

ISBN: 9781548317560
Category: Children's/ Middle Grade/ Educational/ Interactive with comprehension/ Anti-Bullying
Polly the Baby Parrot is abducted by Two-legged Destroyers from her home in Africa and sent to a pet shop in Scotland. There, Child - Two-legged Destroyers, tease and bully her. Then, one day in walks Captain Hake - a Pirate Captain, and rescues her. Polly the Baby Parrot meets Jolly Roger the Rat and they become good friends. One day they play a game of Hide and Seek...

Polly Finds Treasure

ISBN: 978-0-9947238-1-9
Category: Children's/ Middle Grade/ Educational/ Interactive with comprehension/Adventure/ Pirates
Captain Hake and his crew come across the deserted Queen Anne's Revenge – Captain Blackbeard's ship. The crew accidentally trip the booby traps and awakens the ghost of Captain Blackbeard and his crew and have to fight for their lives to escape. They find a map in a bottle and sail to Skull Island in search of treasure...

Polly's Piralympics

ISBN: 978-1537543079
Category: Children's/ Middle Grade/ Educational/ Interactive with comprehension/ Pirates/ Disabilities/ Anti-Bullying
Polly the Parrot has the idea of sharing their last bounty of prosthetic arms, blades and racing wheelchairs with their crew and those of the other pirate ships. They challenge the other pirates to a Piralympic Games, (Paralympics for Pirates.) Follow the vuvuzela playing Zulus; kilted bagpipe playing Scots; tattooed Maoris; and the other pirate crews, as they compete for Captain Kingklip's locker of GOLD doubloons.

Polly's Inuit Piralympics

ISBN: 978-0-620-74968-8

Category: Children's/ Middle Grade/ Educational/ Interactive with comprehension/ Other Cultures/ Adventure

Polly the Parrot fly's north to the land of snow and ice, as our old favourites are joined by the GIRLS - the Greek Goddesses and the Japanese Ninjas. This time, the pirate crews take part in the Inuit (Eskimo) Piralympics. They build Igloos, create ice sculptures and take part in a sled race that nearly ends in disaster...

Polly's Rainy-Day Piralympics

ISBN:

Category: Children's/ Middle Grade/ Educational/ Interactive with comprehension/ Other Cultures/ Adventure/ Disabilities

Polly the Parrot is joined by Nessie the Loch Ness Monster as they head to Ireland for the Rainy-Day Piralympics (Indoor Paralympics for Pirates). Meet a new crew, sailing an unusual vessel. Find out about Pollyopolly, and be on the lookout for those pesky Leprechauns who are out to steal the pirates' GOLD.

Polly's Hogmanay Holiday

ISBN: 978-1979869171

Category: Children's/ Middle Grade/ Educational/ Interactive with comprehension/ Social Awareness

Polly the Parrot, Captain Hake and the crew of the Thistle take a short break in Scotland before they resume their search for Polly's friends in Africa. The pirates get to meet the street children and their lives are changed forever. Red relates how the Sweetie Man gives out drugs. But who is Red? And what happens to the Sweetie Man?

You can follow me at:
http://www.kidsbookswithoutborders.com

https://www.facebook.com/Jann-Weeratunga-Author-721448288028560/

https://www.goodreads.com/jannweeratunga

janspicssa@gmail.com

amazon.com/author/jannweeratunga

Also for younger readers

Toucane is Different

ISBN: 9781723827082
Category: Children's/ Picture and Story Book/ Educational/ Interactive colouring-in.
Toucane the Toucan arrives in Africa after being taken from his home in South America. He searches for a new home, somewhere similar to where he came from, where it is warm all year round. He finds a friend in Mpho the Macaw, but Mpho's family are not so friendly...

Toucane and the Rubbish Rangers

ISBN: 978-1984141507
Category: Children's/ Picture and Story Book/ Educational/ Interactive colouring-in.
Toucane the Toucan and his friend Mpho the Macaw are watching the humans playing volleyball, surfing and sunbathing. Then, one of the humans drops some litter and Toucane the Toucan can't restrain himself any longer. Learn how Toucane the Toucan and the Rubbish Ranger clean up our environment...

Toucane Warns of Stranger Danger

ISBN: 9781790216208
Category: Children's/ Picture and Story Book/ Educational/ Interactive colouring-in.
Toucane the Toucan and Mpho the Macaw go on holiday. On the way, they meet Toucane's old friends. Once at the beach, Toucane the Toucan spots his old owner and flies down to greet him. Ntsika is very happy to see Toucane. Ntsika is with his family and his friends. Their children go off to get ice creams, but Keats runs ahead and is grabbed by the Shady Lady...

ABOUT THE AUTHOR

Jann Weeratunga was born in London in 1963. She has lived and worked in London, UK: Sri Lanka: UAE and Bahrain. Currently, she lives in Johannesburg, South Africa with her four fur babies.

She was a Primary School Teacher and a Scout/Cub Leader for over 20 years and now visits schools giving workshops on writing books, as well as anti-bullying talks.

She has written four children's book series, including: the Polly's Piralympics Series, the Toucane Series and the Hettie Series

The Polly's Piralympics series was inspired by the closing ceremony of the 2012 London Paralympic Games. In his closing speech, Sir Phillip Craven told of how a young boy was reading with his mother. In the book, he saw a man with an eye patch, a hook for a hand, a parrot on his shoulder and a wooden leg.

When asked who it was, he said:

"Well, he has only one leg, so he must be an Olympian."

Such was the strength of the London 2012 Paralympics that it changed peoples' perceptions of disability forever. The speech made her both laugh and cry and gave her the inspiration for this series of books, which are both unique in concept as well as content.

The Toucane Series, for younger readers 5-8 year-olds, are stand-alone stories, with colouring pages and a song.

The Hettie Series ages 3-6 are colouring-in books with a simple story.

Made in the USA
Columbia, SC
23 April 2022